Advance Praise for
The Essence of Tsongkhapa's Teachings

"When I first studied Jé Tsongkhapa's root text on the *Three Principal Aspects of the Path* several decades ago, I recognized I had encountered the essence of all the Mahāyāna teachings of the Buddha, and the indispensable foundation of the Vajrayāna. I knew that I could entrust myself to these three principles in all my lifetimes until enlightenment, and my faith in them has only deepened during the ensuing years. In this precious volume, His Holiness the Dalai Lama has brought his vast erudition and profound insights to elucidating this text for the modern world, for which I offer my humble gratitude and joyful appreciation."
    —B. Alan Wallace, president, Santa Barbara Institute
                            for Consciousness Studies

"I teach my students about bodhisattva practice in terms of the three main aspects of the path: determination to be free, bodhichitta, and correct view. I am thrilled to see that we now have Tsongkhapa's pithy and profound verses on this topic along with the Dalai Lama's lucid commentary. This is a short, readable book—and a great introduction to Mahāyāna practice. It includes Tsongkhapa's original text in Tibetan, so it could also be used quite effectively as a text for teaching the translation of classical Tibetan."
    —Guy Newland, chair, Department of Philosophy and
                    Religion, Central Michigan University

The Essence of
Tsongkhapa's Teachings

❧

The Dalai Lama on
The Three Principal Aspects
of the Path

Translated by Ven. Lhakdor

and

Edited by Jeremy Russell

WISDOM PUBLICATIONS
IN COLLABORATION WITH THE
LIBRARY OF TIBETAN WORKS & ARCHIVES

Wisdom Publications
199 Elm Street
Somerville, MA 02144 USA
wisdompubs.org

Library of Congress Cataloging-in-Publication Data
Names: Bstan-ʾdzin-rgya-mtsho, Dalai Lama XIV, 1935– author. |
    Lhakdor, translator. | Russell, Jeremy, editor. | Tsong-kha-pa Blo-bzang-
    grags-pa, 1357–1419. Lam gyi gtso bo rnam gsum. | Tsong-kha-pa Blo-
    bzang-grags-pa, 1357–1419. Lam gyi gtso bo rnam gsum. English.
Title: The essence of Tsongkhapa's teachings: the Dalai Lama on the three
    principal aspects of the path / by His Holiness the XIV Dalai Lama;
    translated by Ven. Lhakdor and edited by Jeremy Russell.
Description: Somerville, MA: Wisdom Publications, 2019. | Series:
    Library of Tibetan works and archives | Includes bibliographical refer-
    ences. | Identifiers: LCCN 2018029703 (print) |
    LCCN 2018055279 (ebook) | ISBN 9781614295945 (ebook) |
    ISBN 9781614295693 (pbk.: alk. paper)
Subjects: LCSH: Tsong-kha-pa Blo-bzang-grags-pa, 1357–1419. Lam gyi
    gtso bo rnam gsum. | Lam-rim. | Spiritual life—Dge-lus-pa (Sect)
Classification: LCC BQ7950.T754 (ebook) | LCC BQ7950.T754 L323
    2019 (print) | DDC 294.3/444—dc23
LC record available at https://lccn.loc.gov/2018029703

ISBN 978-1-61429-569-3   ebook ISBN 978-1-61429-594-5

22 21 20 19 18   5 4 3 2 1

Cover design by Gopa&Ted2. Interior design by Partners Composition.
Set in DGP 11.5 pt./14.5 pt. and Qomolangma Title 14 pt./24 pt.

Wisdom Publications' books are printed on acid-free paper and meet the
guidelines for permanence and durability of the Production Guidelines for
Book Longevity of the Council on Library Resources.

♻ This book was produced with environmental mindfulness. For more
information, please visit wisdompubs.org/wisdom-environment.

Printed in Canada.

Contents

Preface

I am happy that Wisdom Publications is publishing His Holiness the Dalai Lama's commentary on *Three Principal Aspects of the Path*, by Jé Tsongkhapa, which I had the fortune to simultaneously translate during the teaching itself, and later prepare this written translation for the Library of Tibetan Works and Archives (LTWA) with the help of my friend Jeremy Russell. Tsongkhapa taught this short text to Tsakho Onpo Ngawang Dakpa in a place called Gyamo Rong in eastern Tibet.

The three principal aspects of the path are the axis or lifeline of all the sutric and tantric practices that you undertake. In other words, it is important that your practice be influenced by the three aspects: renunciation or the determination to be free, bodhichitta or the mind of enlightenment, and right or correct view. For when your practice is influenced by renunciation it becomes a cause for achieving liberation (nirvana), when it is influenced by bodhichitta it becomes a cause for achieving omniscience (buddhahood), and when it is influenced by correct view it becomes an antidote to the cycle of existence (samsara). In the absence of these main aspects of the path, even if one is well versed in the five subjects of learning, even if one is able to remain in a meditative state for many eons, even if one possesses the five clairvoyances, and even if one has achieved the eight great accomplishments, one will not be able to go beyond this cycle of existence.

The three principal aspects of the path are the essence of all the scriptures of the Buddha. The meaning of the Buddha's teachings and the commentaries on them are included in the stages of the path of three types of individuals—the lowest, who is concerned with a higher rebirth; the medium, who is concerned with liberation or nirvana; and the highest-capacity individual, who is concerned with the bodhisattva motivation of becoming a buddha to benefit other beings. This is so because the purpose of all the scriptures containing the Buddha's teachings and their commentaries is really to help followers achieve buddhahood. To attain that state of omniscience, one should practice the twofold practice of skillful means and wisdom, within which the main practice is bodhichitta and correct view (wisdom understanding emptiness). In order to cultivate these two, one should have first of all cultivated a deep sense of disgust toward the superficial marvels of the cycle of existence, and should have developed genuine renunciation—the wish to come out of samsara. In the absence of this, it is impossible to develop the great compassion that aspires to liberate other sentient beings from the cycle of existence. Hence renunciation is a must.

Bodhichitta is the main practice of accumulation of merit for achieving the body of the Buddha (rupakaya), and correct view is the main practice for achieving the truth body (dharmakaya). Moreover, in the beginning, in order to convince one's mind to embrace Dharma, one needs renunciation. To ensure that the Dharma practice becomes a Mahayana path of practice, one needs bodhichitta, and to eliminate completely the two obscurations, correct view is a must. Thus these three are known as the three principal aspects of the path. This way of practicing all the essential points of the path by including them in these three principal aspects is a very special instruction that Manjushri gave directly to Tsongkhapa.

Ven. Lhakdor, Director, LTWA

Part 1

ལམ་གཙོ་རྣམ་གསུམ།

Three Principal Aspects of the Path
by Jé Tsongkhapa

༄༅། །རྗེ་བཙུན་བླ་མ་རྣམས་ལ་ཕྱག་འཚལ་ལོ། །

རྒྱལ་བའི་གསུང་རབ་ཀུན་གྱི་སྙིང་པོའི་དོན། །

རྒྱལ་སྲས་དམ་པ་རྣམས་ཀྱིས་བསྔགས་པའི་ལམ། །

སྐལ་ལྡན་ཐར་འདོད་རྣམས་ཀྱི་འཇུག་ངོགས་དེ། །

ཇི་ལྟར་ནུས་བཞིན་བདག་གིས་བཤད་པར་བྱ། །

གང་དག་སྲིད་པའི་བདེ་ལ་མ་ཆགས་ཤིང༌། །

དལ་འབྱོར་དོན་ཡོད་བྱ་ཕྱིར་བརྩོན་པ་ཡིས། །

རྒྱལ་བ་དགྱེས་པའི་ལམ་ལ་ཡིད་རྟོན་པའི། །

སྐལ་ལྡན་དེ་དག་དང་བའི་ཡིད་ཀྱིས་ཉོན། །

I pay homage to the foremost venerable lamas

I will explain, as well as I can,
the essence of all the teachings of the Conqueror,
the path praised by the Conqueror's children,
the entrance for the fortunate desiring liberation.

Those who are not attached to the joys of the cyclic
    existence,
who strive to make meaning of this leisure and opportunity,
who rely on the path pleasing to the Conqueror—
those fortunate ones, listen with a clear mind.

རྣམ་དག་རིས་འབྱུང་མེད་པར་སྟེང་མཚོ་ཡི། །
བདེ་འབྲས་དོན་གཉེར་ཞི་བའི་ཐབས་མེད་ལ། །
སྲིད་ལ་བཀུམ་པ་ཡིས་ཀྱང་ལུས་ཅན་རྣམས། །
ཀུན་ནས་འཆིང་ཕྱིར་ཐོག་མར་རིས་འབྱུང་བཙལ། །

དལ་འབྱོར་རྙེད་དཀའ་ཚེ་ལ་ལོང་མེད་པ། །
ཡིད་ལ་གོམས་པས་ཚེ་འདིའི་སྣང་ཤས་ལྡོག །
ལས་འབྲས་མི་བསླུ་འཁོར་བའི་སྡུག་བསྔལ་རྣམས། །
ཡང་ཡང་བསམས་པས་ཕྱི་མའི་སྣང་ཤས་ལྡོག །

Without a pure determination to be free,
there is no means to achieve peace owing to fixation
    on the pleasurable effects of the ocean of existence.
Embodied beings are thoroughly bound by craving for
    existence;
therefore, in the beginning, seek a determination to be
    free.

Contemplating how freedom and fortune are difficult
    to find,
and that in life there is no time to waste, blocks the
    attraction to the captivating appearances of this life.
Repeatedly contemplating actions' infallible effects,
and the sufferings of cyclic existence, blocks the
    captivating appearance of future lives.

དེ་ལྟར་གོམས་པས་འཁོར་བའི་ཕུན་ཚོགས་ལ། །
ཡིད་སྨོན་སྐད་ཅིག་ཙམ་ཡང་མི་སྐྱེ་ཞིང་། །
ཉིན་མཚན་ཀུན་ཏུ་ཐར་པ་དོན་གཉེར་བློ། །
བྱུང་ན་དེ་ཚེ་ངེས་འབྱུང་སྐྱེས་པ་ལགས། །

ངེས་འབྱུང་དེ་ཡང་རྣམ་དག་སེམས་བསྐྱེད་ཀྱིས། །
ཟིན་པ་མེད་ན་བླ་མེད་བྱང་ཆུབ་ཀྱི། །
ཕུན་ཚོགས་བདེ་བའི་རྒྱུ་རུ་མི་འགྱུར་བས། །
བློ་ལྡན་རྣམས་ཀྱིས་བྱང་ཆུབ་སེམས་མཆོག་བསྐྱེད། །

Having familiarized yourself in this way,
if you do not generate admiration
for the prosperity of cyclic existence even for an instant,
and if you wish for liberation day and night,
at that time you have generated the determination to
    be free.

If this determination to be free is not influenced
by a pure mind of enlightenment,
it will not become a cause for unsurpassable enlightenment,
    the perfect bliss;
therefore the intelligent should generate a mind of
    enlightenment.

ཕྱགས་དག་ཆུ་བོ་བཞི་ཡི་རྒྱུན་གྱིས་ཁྱེར། །
བསྒོག་དཀའ་ལས་ཀྱི་འཆིང་བ་དམ་པོས་བསྡམས། །
བདག་འཛིན་ལྕགས་ཀྱི་དྲ་བའི་སྦུབས་སུ་ཚུད། །
མ་རིག་མུན་པའི་སྨག་ཆེན་ཀུན་ནས་འཐིབས། །

ཀུ་མེད་སྲིད་པར་སྐྱེ་ཞིང་སྐྱེ་བ་རུ། །
སྡུག་བསྔལ་གསུམ་གྱིས་རྒྱུན་ཆད་མེད་པར་མནར། །
གནས་སྐབས་འདི་འདྲར་གྱུར་པའི་མ་རྣམས་ཀྱི། །
ངང་ཚུལ་བསམས་ནས་སེམས་མཆོག་བསྐྱེད་པར་མཛོད། །

Carried away by the four torrential rivers,
bound by tight bonds of actions, difficult to undo,
caught in the iron net of the conception of self,
thoroughly enveloped by the thick darkness of
  ignorance . . .

born into boundless cyclic existence,
and in rebirths unceasingly tormented by the three
  sufferings—
contemplating the state of mother sentient beings in
  such conditions, generate the supreme mind.
Seeing the sufferings of the mother sentient beings that
  are in such a situation,
we should generate the supreme mind.

གནས་ལུགས་རྟོགས་པའི་ཤེས་རབ་མི་ལྡན་ན། །
ངེས་འབྱུང་བྱང་ཆུབ་སེམས་ལ་གོམས་བྱས་ཀྱང་། །
སྲིད་པའི་རྩ་བ་བཅད་པར་མི་ནུས་པས། །
དེ་ཕྱིར་རྟེན་འབྲེལ་རྟོགས་པའི་ཐབས་ལ་འབད། །

གང་ཞིག་འཁོར་འདས་ཆོས་རྣམས་ཐམས་ཅད་ཀྱི། །
རྒྱུ་འབྲས་ནམ་ཡང་བསླུ་བ་མེད་མཐོང་ཞིང་། །
དམིགས་པའི་གཏད་སོ་གང་ཡིན་ཀུན་ཞིག་པ། །
དེ་ནི་སངས་རྒྱས་དགྱེས་པའི་ལམ་ལ་ཞུགས། །

Without the wisdom realizing the ultimate nature of
    existence,
even though you familiarize yourself with the determina-
    tion to be free and the mind of enlightenment,
the root of cyclic existence cannot be cut;
therefore make an effort to realize dependent arising.

One who sees the infallible cause and effect
of all phenomena in cyclic existence and beyond
and destroys all perceptions (of inherent existence)
has entered the path that pleases the Buddha.

སྐྱང་བ་རྗེན་འཁྱལ་བསྐུ་བ་མེད་པ་དང་། །
སྟོང་པ་ཁས་ལེན་བྱལ་བའི་གོ་བ་གཉིས། །
ཇི་སྲིད་སོ་སོར་སྣང་བ་དེ་སྲིད་དུ། །
ད་དུང་ཐུབ་པའི་དགོངས་པ་རྟོགས་པ་མེད། །

ནམ་ཞིག་རེས་འཇོག་མེད་པར་ཅིག་ཅར་དུ། །
རྟེན་འཁྱལ་མི་བསྐུར་མཐོང་བ་ཙམ་ཉིད་ནས། །
རིས་ཤེས་ཡུལ་གྱི་འཛིན་སྟངས་ཀུན་ཞིག་ན། །
དེ་ཚེ་ལྟ་བའི་དཔྱད་པ་རྫོགས་པ་ལགས། །

Appearances are infallible dependent arisings;
emptiness is free of assertions.
As long as these two understandings are seen as
  separate,
one has not yet realized the intent of the Buddha.

At the time when these two realizations are
  simultaneous and don't have to alternate,
from the mere sight of infallible dependent arising
  comes ascertainment
that completely destroys all modes of grasping;
at that time, the analysis of the profound view is complete.

གནས་ཡང་སྐྱང་བས་ཡོད་མཐའ་སེལ་བ་དང་། །

སྟོང་པས་མེད་མཐའ་སེལ་ཞིང་སྟོང་པ་ཉིད། །

རྒྱུ་དང་འབྲས་བུར་འཆར་བའི་ཚུལ་ཤེས་ན། །

མཐར་འཛིན་ལྟ་བས་འཕྲོག་པར་མི་འགྱུར་རོ། །

དེ་ལྟར་ལམ་གྱི་གཙོ་བོ་རྣམ་གསུམ་གྱི། །

གནད་རྣམས་རང་གིས་ཇི་བཞིན་རྟོགས་པའི་ཚེ། །

དབེན་པ་བསྟེན་ཏེ་བརྩོན་འགྲུས་སྟོབས་བསྐྱེད་ནས། །

གཏན་གྱི་འདུན་མ་མྱུར་དུ་སྒྲུབས་ཤིག་བུ། །

ཞེས་པ་འདི་ནི་མང་དུ་ཐོས་པའི་དགེ་སློང་བློ་བཟང་གྲགས་པའི་དཔལ་གྱིས་ཚ་ཁོ་དབོན་
པོ་ངག་དབང་གྲགས་པ་ལ་གདམས་པའོ། །

Also, when the extreme of existence is eliminated by
    appearances,
and the extreme of nonexistence is eliminated by
    emptiness,
and the nature of the arising of cause and effect from
    emptiness is known,
you will not be captivated by the view that grasps at
    extremes.

Thus when you have realized the essentials
of the three principal aspects of the path, accordingly,
seek solitude and generate the power of effort,
and quickly actualize your ultimate purpose, my son.

*The text is taught by Jé Tsongkhapa to Tsakho Onpo Ngawang
Dakpa.*

Part 2

Introduction

by His Holiness the Dalai Lama

Today I am going to explain the *Three Principal Aspects of the Path*. As usual, before beginning a teaching, we will do the three practices for cleaning our mental continuums and then we will recite the *Heart Sutra*. Now make the mandala offering.

Whatever teachings are being given, both the listener and the teacher should have a pure motivation. Especially when listening to a Mahayana teaching, you should first take refuge in the Buddha, Dharma, and Sangha to protect yourself from following the wrong path, and second you should generate an altruistic mind of enlightenment to differentiate yourself from followers of lower paths. Therefore we should visualize two points: first, taking refuge in the Buddha, Dharma, and Sangha for the benefit of all sentient beings, then generating the altruistic aspiration to enlightenment for the sake of all sentient beings. So with this motivation, we should recite the verse for taking refuge in the Buddha, Dharma, and Sangha three times, clearly visualizing that we are doing so for the benefit of all sentient beings.

After the incomparable Buddha had attained enlightenment at the Bodh Gaya, he taught the four noble truths: the truth of suffering, the true causes of suffering, the true cessation of suffering, and the true path. This became the basis or foundation for all the later teachings he gave. Although the Buddha taught the four noble truths during his first turning of the wheel of the doctrine, the meaning of true cessation was most explicitly taught during the second turning of the wheel of doctrine. At that time he taught the meaning of emptiness directly and the stages of the path implicitly. In other words, while teaching emptiness directly, he taught the meaning of the two truths—conventional and ultimate truth—and the complete meaning of nirvana and cessation.

During the third turning of the wheel of doctrine, the Buddha taught the meaning of Buddha nature in the *Tathagata Essence Sutra*, which forms the basis for Maitreya's *Sublime Science* (*Uttaratantra*). He explained that sentient beings have a buddha nature or an ability to become enlightened mainly in terms of the nature of the mind, which is empty of inherent existence and thus suitable to be transformed into enlightenment. It is clearly explained in *Sublime Science* that the mind is by nature pure and free of defilement, which makes it suitable for attaining enlightenment. This is because anything that lacks inherent existence is changeable and subject to causes and conditions. As Nagarjuna says in *Fundamental Wisdom of the Middle Way*:

> For whichever (system) emptiness is possible, for
>   that (system) all is possible.
> For whichever (system) emptiness is not possible,
>   for that (system) nothing is possible.

The meaning of the term "emptiness" is "empty of inherent existence," and that means being dependent on something else, being dependent on causes and conditions. When we say that something is dependent on other phenomena, it means that when those phenomena change, that particular thing will also change. If it were not dependent on something else and had inherent existence, then it would not be subject to change due to other conditions.

So during the second turning of the wheel of doctrine, teaching that phenomena lack inherent existence, the Buddha taught that phenomena can be made to change because they are dependent on causes and conditions. Now, although phenomena lack inherent existence when they appear to us, we think that they exist inherently. Not only do phenomena appear as if they are inherently existent, but we also become attached to them and determine that they exist inherently. In this way, we generate craving, desire, anger, and so forth. When we encounter some pleasant or interesting object, we generate a lot of attachment, and if we see something distasteful or unappealing, we get angry. Therefore problems like anger and attachment arise because of conceiving phenomena as inherently existent.

The conception of phenomena as inherently existent is a wrong consciousness mistaken toward its referent object, which provides the foundation for all delusions. However, if we generate an understanding that phenomena are not inherently existent, it will act as a counterforce to that wrong consciousness. This shows that the defilements of the mind can be removed. If the delusions that defile the mind are removable, then the seeds or potencies left behind by these delusions can also be eliminated. The absolute purity of the mind, which is its lack of inherent existence, is taught explicitly in the second turning of the wheel of the doctrine. During the third turning of the wheel, it is explained again not only from the ultimate but also from the conventional point of view that the ultimate nature of the mind is pure, and in its pure state it is only neutral and clear light.

For example, whoever we are, delusions do not manifest within us all the time. What is more, we sometimes generate anger and sometimes generate love even toward the same object, which ought not to be possible if things have inherent existence. This clearly shows that the real nature of the principal mind, the mind itself, is pure, but due to mental factors or the minds that accompany the principal mind, it sometimes appears to have a virtuous quality like love and at other times appears in a deluded form like anger. The nature of the principal mind is therefore neutral, but being dependent on its accompanying mind, it may change from a virtuous to a nonvirtuous mind.

So the mind by nature is clear light and the defilements or delusions are temporary and adventitious. This indicates that if we practice and cultivate virtuous qualities, the mind can be transformed positively. On the other hand, if the mind encounters delusions, then it will take on the form of delusions. Therefore all such qualities as the ten powers of the Buddha can also be attained because of this quality of the mind.

For example, all the different kinds of consciousness have the same quality of understanding and knowing their object clearly, but when a particular consciousness encounters some obstacle, it may not be able to understand its object. Although my eye consciousness has the potential to see an object, if I cover it up it will be obstructed from seeing the object. Similarly, consciousness may not be able to see the object because it is too far away. So the mind already has the potential to understand all phenomena, a quality that need not be strengthened but that may be obstructed by other factors.

With the attainment of the higher qualities of a buddha, like the ten powers, we attain a full state of consciousness able to see the object clearly and completely. This state of consciousness can be attained merely by recognizing the real nature of the mind and removing the delusions and obstructions from it.

During the third turning of the wheel of the doctrine, of the four noble truths initially taught during the first turning of the wheel, the meaning of the true path is explained clearly by defining the meaning of *tathagatagarbha*, or Buddha nature. Buddha nature makes possible the attainment of omniscience, the ultimate state of consciousness able to see phenomena and their ultimate mode of being.

Therefore a complete explanation of the meaning of true cessation is given during the second turning of the wheel of the doctrine and a detailed explanation of the true path is given during the third turning of the wheel. They explain the mind's potential to know the ultimate mode of existence of phenomena and how omniscience can be achieved if you promote and develop that potential.

Now, when it comes to explaining the ultimate nature of the mind and its suitability for attaining enlightenment, we have the accounts of both sutra and tantra. These are differentiated by the details of their explanation of the nature of the mind. The tantric teachings give a clear explanation of the subtlest state of enlightenment within the highest class of tantra—that is, Highest Yoga Tantra. The first three classes of tantra form a foundation for that Highest Yoga Tantra.

In essence, this is a brief explanation of the Buddha's teaching from the four noble truths up to the highest class of tantric teaching. However, even if we have a clear understanding of the ultimate nature of the mind and the possibility of attaining enlightenment with it, if we do not practice and make effort to achieve that goal, then enlightenment will not be attainable. So while on the one hand it is important to know the ultimate nature of the mind, on the other, we should generate an intention to practice and realize this potential.

In teaching the first two noble truths the Buddha described the faults, the defects that must be given up and eliminated—that is, true suffering and the true origin of suffering. In teaching the second pair of the four noble truths—that is, the true path and true cessation—the Buddha explained that there is a method, a path to get rid of these sufferings and delusions through which the complete cessation of those delusions can be attained. If there were no cure or method to eliminate suffering and attain a state of complete cessation and peace, it would not be necessary to think about, discuss, or meditate on suffering because doing so would merely engender pessimism and create more suffering for yourself. It would be better to remain bewildered and carefree. However, we do have a chance, there is path and method to get rid of suffering, so it is worthwhile to think and talk about suffering. This is the importance and encompassing quality of the Buddha's teaching of the four noble truths, for they provide the basis and foundation of all practices.

When we think about suffering and the true origin of suffering, and we come to an understanding of these two truths, we will generate a wish to rid ourselves of suffering and its causes. In other words, because we dislike true suffering and know the true origin of suffering we will generate a wish to reject them. This is called the determination to be free.

When you carefully consider suffering, it is not only you who are under its power, for other sentient beings also suffer in the same way. Then you should think that as other sentient beings are suffering just like me, how marvelous it would be if they could also eliminate suffering and its causes. Such a wish for other sentient beings to eliminate suffering and its causes is called compassion. When, induced by compassion, you decide that you will help them eliminate suffering and its causes, that is the special resolve or the mind that wishes actively to benefit other sentient beings.

Then if you look carefully at how sentient beings can be benefited not just temporarily but ultimately, you will conclude that you will be able to benefit them completely only if you help them attain enlightenment, and to do that you must attain enlightenment yourself. This compassionate mind wishing to attain buddhahood in order to help all sentient beings attain enlightenment is called the mind of enlightenment.

Because phenomena do not have an independent or inherent existence, it is feasible to get rid of suffering and attain the ultimate status of enlightenment. Therefore it is important to understand the nature of phenomena, its lack of inherent existence. This understanding of phenomena's lack of inherent existence is called right view.

It is these three qualities—the determination to be free, the mind of enlightenment, and right or correct view—that are treated here as the three principal paths. They are so called because they provide the real motivation for attaining liberation from cyclic existence and form the framework for attaining enlightenment.

The principal means of attaining liberation from cyclic existence is the determination to be free, and the principal means of attaining enlightenment is the mind of enlightenment. Both of these are augmented by right view or wisdom realizing emptiness.

Now I will begin to explain the text.

Part 3

The Teachings

THE HOMAGE

I pay homage to the foremost venerable lamas

This line is the author's expression of respect before composing the text. I will explain the meaning of the words here. The term *lama* not only denotes a position of status and power in the mundane sense but also indicates someone who is truly kind and possesses immense qualities. The Tibetan word *Jey*, or "foremost," here signifies someone who cares less about the immediate or sensual pleasures of this world, this life in cyclic existence, than for the next life. It refers to someone who is more concerned about other sentient beings' long-term benefit over many lives to come. The Tibetan word *tsun*, meaning "venerable" or "disciplined," refers to the lama because he has understood that, however pleasing or attractive they might be, the pleasures and attractions of cyclic existence are worthless. He has seen the lack of any lasting value in worldly phenomena and has turned his mind toward the longer-lasting happiness of future lives. In other words, the lama is one who has disciplined his mind and is not hankering after the delights of this world but aspires for the attainment of liberation. The word *lama* actually means "supreme," indicating one who has greater care for other sentient beings than for himself and neglects his own interests for their sake. "I pay homage" implies bowing down. You bow down to the lama on seeing his quality of concern for other sentient beings and their happiness at the cost of his own. In paying respect to this quality in the lama, by bowing down to him, you make an aspiration to attain such qualities yourself.

The Promise to Compose the Text

**(1) I will explain, as well as I can,
the essence of all the teachings of the
Conqueror,
the path praised by the Conqueror's children,
the entrance for the fortunate desiring
liberation.**

The first line expresses the author's promise to compose the text. The second implies the determination to be free, because all the Buddha's teachings aim toward liberation. It is from this point of view—the attainment of liberation—that we should be able to see faults in the attractions of cyclic existence and generate a wish to renounce those attractions. Renunciation is imperative if we wish to achieve liberation. So this line implies renunciation of cyclic existence. The phrase "Conqueror's children" in the third line has three connotations. It can refer to those born from the Buddha's body, speech, or mind; Rahula was his physical son. The offspring of his speech would be the hearers and solitary buddhas. But in this context, the reference is to those born from the mind of the Buddha, those who have generated the mind of enlightenment. You become a bodhisattva or child of the Buddha only if you have this altruistic aspiration for enlightenment. Bodhisattvas are called offspring of the Buddha's mind because they are born from qualities found in the mindstream of the buddhas.

The last line of the verse implies right view, as the attainment of liberation is dependent on whether you have realized emptiness. So these three lines introduce the three principal aspects of the path—the determination to be free, the mind of enlightenment, and view of emptiness—whose meanings are explained in this text.

Exhorting the Disciples to Listen

**(2) Those who are not attached to the joys
of the cyclic existence,
who strive to make meaning of this leisure
and opportunity,
who rely on the path pleasing to the
Conqueror—
those fortunate ones, listen with a clear
mind.**

Most of us have sufficient resources so we do not have to work very much to obtain food, clothing, and so forth. But it is clear that in this life merely having enough to eat is not sufficiently satisfying. We want something else. We still yearn for something more. This clearly indicates that unless pleasure and happiness are brought about through transforming the mind, it is not possible to achieve lasting happiness through external means, however favorable the external conditions may be. Happiness and discomfort are very much dependent on our mental attitude. So it is important that we should bring about some internal transformation of the mind. Since lasting happiness can only be attained in this way, it is important to rely on the power of mind and to discover the mind's ultimate nature.

There are many diverse teachings in different religious traditions on how to bring about such a transformation. The Buddha's teaching, which we are discussing here, contains a very clear, detailed, and systematic explanation.

We more or less qualify as "those fortunate ones" referred to in this verse because we are trying to reduce our attachment, trying to make meaningful use of this precious life as a free and fortunate human being, and relying on the teachings of the Buddha. So this line tells us to pay attention to the teaching that the author is going to impart.

Need to Generate the Determination to Be Free

**(3) Without a pure determination to be free,
there is no means to achieve peace owing
    to fixation on the pleasurable effects of
    the ocean of existence.
Embodied beings are thoroughly bound
    by craving for existence;
therefore, in the beginning, seek a
    determination to be free.**

Here we begin the body of the text, the actual teaching it contains. This verse explains the necessity of generating a determination to be free or a mind seeking a release from cyclic existence. Seeing the faults and shortcomings of cyclic existence and generating a strong wish to abandon it and attain liberation is called a determination to be free. As long as you are unable to see the worthlessness of the pleasures of the cyclic existence, but continue to see some meaning or attraction in them and cling to them, you will not be able to turn your mind toward liberation or realize how you are bound.

So the first line of this verse says that unless you have a pure determination to free yourself from the ocean of cyclic existence, your attempts to achieve peace will be in vain. It is our fascination with cyclic existence owing to craving and attachment that binds us within it. Therefore, if we really seek the peace of liberation, the right course to adopt is to generate the determination to be free, to recognize the faults of cyclic existence and reject them. The biography of the Buddha himself can provide us with a clear understanding of the meaning of the determination to be free for our own practice.

He was born a prince in a wealthy family, was well educated, had a wife and son, and enjoyed all imaginable worldly pleasures. Yet despite all the alluring pleasures available to him, when he came across instances of the sufferings of birth, sickness, old age, and death, he was provoked by the sight of the suffering of others. He discovered for himself that, no matter how attractive external comforts may be, so long as you have a physical body like ours, which is the short-lived product of contaminated action and delusion, then such attractive external pleasures are illusory. Understanding this, he tried to find a path to liberation from suffering by renouncing all worldly pleasures, including family life with his wife and son. Through gradually increasing his determination to be free in this way, he was able to attain not only liberation but also enlightenment.

Therefore it is taught that we need to develop a determination to be free. Merely renouncing the comforts of cyclic existence and checking attachment and craving toward it are not enough. We must cut the stream of births. Rebirth comes about because of craving and desire, and we must cut its continuity through the practice of meditation. Hence the Buddha entered into deep meditative stabilization for six years. Finally, by means of a union of calm abiding and special insight, he attained the power to overcome the hindrances presented by the aggregates and external evil forces. He eliminated the very source of disturbing emotions, and because they were extinguished he also overcame death. In this way he conquered all four evil forces or hindrances.

As followers of the Buddha, we too should try to see faults in the alluring attractions of cyclic existence. Then, without attachment toward them, generate concentration and focus on the view of selflessness, understanding the real nature of phenomena.

How to Generate the
Determination to Be Free

Now, should you wonder how to practice this determination to be free, how to generate a mind that wishes to renounce cyclic existence, the next verse says:

> (4) Contemplating how freedom and
>   fortune are difficult to find,
> and that in life there is no time to waste,
>   blocks the attraction to the captivating
>   appearances of this life.
> Repeatedly contemplating actions' infallible
>   effects,
> and the sufferings of cyclic existence,
>   blocks the captivating appearance
>   of future lives.

This verse explains how to check attachment first to this life and then toward future lives. In order to cut attachment toward the pleasures of this life, it is important to think about the preciousness of this human life, how it is difficult to find and the many qualities it provides. If we think clearly about these points, we will be able to extract meaning from having attained a human birth. Life as a human being is precious because with it we attain a status, quality, and intelligence that is absent in all other animals, even in all other sentient beings. We have the power to achieve great benefit and destruction. If we were to just while away our time and waste this precious potential in silly and meaningless activities, it would be a great loss.

Therefore it is important that we recognize our capacity, our qualities, and our supreme intelligence, which other sentient beings do not possess. If we can identify these things, we will be able to appreciate and use them. The power of the human brain and human intelligence is marvelous. It is capable of planning ahead and can engage in deep and extensive thought, as other species of sentient beings cannot do. Since we have such a powerful brain or intelligence, it is important that we first recognize the strength and character of its attribute of awareness. We should then steer our awareness in the right direction, so that it can contribute significantly to peace and harmony in the world and within all sentient beings.

Let us take the example of nuclear energy. There is great power within a nuclear particle, but if we use that power wrongly or mishandle it, it can be very destructive. Nowadays we have nuclear missiles and other weapons, the very names of which make us afraid because they are so destructive. They can cause mass destruction in a fraction of time. On the other hand, if we put nuclear power to use in a constructive way, it can be of great service to humanity and sentient beings at large. Similarly, since human beings have such capacity and power, it is very important that they use them for the benefit of all sentient beings. Properly employed, human ingenuity can be a great source of benefit and happiness, but if misused it can bring great misery and destruction.

It is from the point of view of this keen intelligence that we should think about the significance of our precious human life. However, it is also important to understand that the life of a free and fortunate human being is not only meaningful and difficult to find but is also short-lived.

The next two lines say that if we think repeatedly about the infallible connection between causes, our actions, and the sufferings of cyclic existence, we will be able to cut our attachment to the next life. At present we engage in many levels of activity to obtain food, clothing, and a good name. In addition, our experiences in the latter part of our lives are dependent on the actions that we have performed in the earlier part. This is the meaning of actions and results. Although it is not the subtlest interpretation, when we talk about actions and results, actions include any of the things we do in order to obtain any kind of happiness or pleasure. The results are the effects that we achieve thereby. Therefore in the first part of our lives we engage in certain kinds of activity that we think will lead to some kind of happiness or success in the future. Similarly, we engage in certain kinds of action in this life so that we may be able to achieve a good result in our next life. In other words, our experiences in the latter part of our lives are dependent on the actions we have performed in the earlier part of our lives, and our experiences in the future lives, whether pleasant or unpleasant, are dependent on the actions that we have committed in former lives.

These actions are done by either body, speech, or mind, and so are termed physical, verbal, and mental actions. From the point view of the result that they produce, they can be termed wholesome, unwholesome, or neutral actions. Wholesome actions give rise to pleasant results, unwholesome actions give rise to unpleasant results, and neutral actions lead to a feeling of equanimity. Then there are actions that will definitely give rise to a result and those that will not. For example, when an action comes into being, it is motivated, there is an intention, then it is implemented, and finally it is brought to a conclusion.

Now, when the intention, action, and conclusion are all very strong, it is definite that the action will give rise to a result, whether good or bad. On the other hand, if the intention is very strong but you do not put it into effect, or if at the end, instead of thinking that you have completed the deed, you regret what you have done, then that particular action may not produce an effect at that time. If these three aspects—intention, application and conclusion—are not present, the action is classified as indefinite. From the point of view of the basis experiencing the result, there are actions that give fruit in this very life, actions that give fruit in the immediate next life, and actions whose fruits will be experienced in many lives after the next.

Then there are two levels of action that can be classified as projecting and completing actions. Projecting actions are those actions that are responsible for projecting us into a particular life through birth as a human being, animal, or other state of being. Completing actions are those that determine the quality of whatever life you are born into. For example, despite being a human being you may be perpetually poor. Right from birth your sense faculties may be damaged or your limbs crippled. On the other hand, your complexion may be radiant and you may have a natural strength. Even born as an animal you might, like a pet dog, have a comfortable home. These kinds of qualities or defects that you inherit right from birth are the results of completing actions. So a particular action can be termed projecting or completing according to its function. It is possible that although the projecting action is wholesome, the completing action is nonvirtuous, and that although the completing action is unwholesome, the projecting action is virtuous.

Whether a particular action is positive, like faith in the Buddha, or negative, like attachment, if in its own terms it is pure, it can be seen as completely white and virtuous or completely black and unwholesome. If the preparation, application, and conclusion of a particular action are totally virtuous, then that action can be seen as a virtuous action. But if it results from impure preparation, application, and conclusion, then it can be seen as an unwholesome action. If it is a result of a mixed intention, pure application, and impure conclusion—in other words, if it is a mixture of both positive and negative qualities—then it can be called a mixed action.

It is the "I," or the person, who accumulates an action and experiences its results. Although these different levels of actions are the product of the thinking of particular sentient beings, they are not produced by a creator of the world. There is someone who creates the action, because when we talk about action, the world itself clearly implies that there is an actor or agent who performs that action, but it is not an external agent.

How does an action give rise to a result? For example, when I snap my fingers, immediately I stop and the action is complete, leaving behind a result. If you ask what that result is, it is the mere disintegration of the action, and the disintegration of an action goes on continuously. So when we talk about the result of a particular action, it is the mere disintegration, or part of the disintegration, or the cessation of that particular action. To clarify the point, it is a kind of potency left behind by the disintegration of that action, which is responsible for bringing forth many other conditioned phenomena.

If you wonder where the imprints of that potency of the disintegration or cessation of that particular action are left, the answer is on the continuum of the consciousness existing during the immediate moment of the cessation of the action. There are occasions when the consciousness is alert and awake and there are occasions when the consciousness is latent—for example, when we are in deep sleep or when we faint. Therefore the consciousness is not a wholly reliable place to deposit such a potency. Sometimes it is very subtle and sometimes it is very coarse, so the consciousness provides only a temporary basis for such imprints.

Hence if we seek an ultimate explanation, it is the mere "I," or the person, that carries the potency of a particular action. This explanation is based on the ultimate explanation of the highest school—that is, the Middle Way Consequentialist school. I used the phrase "mere I" to clarify that the "I," or the person, has only nominal and not inherent existence. The "I" is only designated and does not exist by itself. It is not something that you can point at with your finger. The word "mere" indicates an "I" that is merely designated by name and thought and negates a self-supporting or independent "I." The negation of an inherently existent or self-supporting "I" does not mean that the "I," or person, becomes the basis on which the imprint or potency of an action is left. In general, the "I" is designated to the collection of physical and mental aggregates.

When we talk about the physical body and consciousness, which are the basis of the designation of the "I" with reference to a human being, it is principally the consciousness that becomes the basis of designation of the term "I." The consciousness has many levels, some of them coarse and some of them subtle. The physical body of a human being can also be divided into many parts, such as the eye, the ear, and so forth. These physical parts again become a basis for the designation of consciousness. For example, the eye consciousness is designated to the eye, the ear consciousness to the ear, and so forth. But if you try to find the subtlest basis of the designation of consciousness, it seems that the nerves and pathways of the brain are actually the basis of the designation of mental consciousness. Then there is also talk of the bases of the sense powers, and these are supposed to be very subtle. It is not clear whether such bases of the sense faculties can be found in the brain or somewhere else. It will be an interesting object of research.

Let us take an example. In order to generate an eye consciousness, many conditions or causes are necessary. The dominant cause is an undefective eye-sense power. Having a particular form within its focus becomes the objective condition. However, despite the presence of such conditions, it is not definite that an eye consciousness will arise. This indicates that a third condition—the immediately preceding condition, which is consciousness—is required in addition to the external objective condition and internal dominant condition of a sense power. Therefore in order for the eye-sense consciousness to arise, all three conditions are necessary.

As an example to elucidate this point, there are occasionally cases of people who, after a long illness, become so physically weak that their heartbeat and all physical functions stop. Since the person has entered into such a deep coma that no physical activity or function can be perceived, the doctor declares them clinically dead. However, sometimes after a few minutes or even hours, despite the apparent lack of physical activity, the person starts breathing again, the heart starts beating, and physical functions are regained. This revival, despite the previous cessation of all physical functions, shows the unavoidable presence of a mental condition that immediately preceded it. When that immediately preceding condition—consciousness—is present, the person can come back to life again. Similarly, in the case of a sense consciousness, the mere presence of the dominant condition and the objective condition is not sufficient to generate a particular consciousness.

According to the Buddhist view, when we talk about the various levels of consciousness of a particular human being that are designated to the various parts of the body, we are referring to the coarser levels of consciousness of a person. These levels of consciousness are called the consciousness of a human being because they are dependent on particular parts of a human body. Therefore when a human being dies, all the coarser levels of consciousness that are dependent on the physical body also seem to disappear, but it is interesting to note that their arising as entities of consciousness does not come about merely because of the presence of the physical body. They are produced as entities of clarity and awareness, such as eye consciousness, ear consciousness, and so forth, in dependence on conditions other than the body. There is a fundamental cause that generates these consciousnesses as entities of clarity and awareness, and according to the various conditions it encounters, consciousnesses cognizing form, sound, and so forth arise. This shows that there is a consciousness independent of the coarser physical body, but when it encounters coarse conditions, it appears in the form of consciousness.

Consciousness has a much subtler nature, and if you examine that subtler nature, then the real, substantial cause of that consciousness can only be another continuum of consciousness that preceded it, irrespective of whether there is a physical body or not. Therefore there is plainly a kind of innate natural mind that is totally pure and clear. When this pure state of the mind comes into contact with different levels of the physical body, consciousness also manifests itself more or less coarsely, depending on what particular physical body it is being designated to. But if you examine the real nature of the mind, it has an existence independent of the coarser levels of the physical body.

Such a pure, natural state of mind, which exists independently of the physical body, is called primordial clear light or the primordial consciousness—a consciousness that has always been present. Compared with this, coarser consciousnesses are adventitious because they are sometimes present and at other times absent. This primordial innate clear light consciousness is the real basis of designation of a sentient being or person. So whoever has this kind of consciousness, this pure state of the mind, is termed a sentient being, and this is the main criterion that differentiates sentient beings from other living things and other phenomena. No doubt a person or "I" is attributed to the total aggregate of the physical body and the consciousness, but it is the primordial innate clear light that is the exclusive basis of the designation of a person, and not the physical body. Even plants and flowers have a kind of physical body, but since they lack this kind of innate subtle consciousness they are not referred to as persons. Whatever your shape, form, or outer aspect, anyone who possesses a continuity of consciousness and has feelings, perception, and so on is referred to as a person. Therefore different texts explain that the "I," or the person, has been attributed to the continuity or stream of consciousness.

Although specific consciousnesses vary according to different occasions and coarser levels of consciousness are dependent on various physical bodies, the subtlest level of consciousness, the mere entity of clarity and awareness—the primordial innate clear light consciousness—is independent of the physical body. The nature of consciousness has no beginning. If you try to trace the origin of consciousness, you can go further and further back, but you will not reach a point at which you can say this is where this consciousness came into being. Therefore it is a kind of natural law that consciousness existed from beginningless time.

This is also a more realistic explanation because if you accept a beginning of consciousness, either you have to assert a creator of consciousness or you have to say that consciousness arises without any cause. This is preposterous, out of concern for which consciousness has been explained as beginningless. If you ask why it is beginningless, we can only say that it is a natural law. If we observe carefully, there are many things in this world whose continuity can be traced from beginningless time. But if you ask what is their real and ultimate origin, you can find no answer. This is simply their nature. If you ask why physical forms appear in the entity of form, it is simply due to their nature. If we say that this comes about without cause or from unrelated causes, then why couldn't it occur causelessly now if it could previously occur without cause?

Therefore, according to the Buddhist view, if you ask whether there is a beginning to consciousness, the answer is that the continuum of consciousness is beginningless, the origin of the "I," or the person, is beginningless, and birth is beginningless. And if you ask whether these things have an end, again the answer is negative if you are thinking about the mere continuum of consciousness or the mere continuum of a person. But there is an end to the impure state of mind, the impure state of a person, and there is also a limit to birth because normally when we talk about birth, we are referring to something that has been produced through contaminated action and delusion.

Because of the beginninglessness of birth, later experiences of suffering and pleasure are connected to actions performed earlier. The different kinds of deluded actions or virtuous actions that a person accumulates in different lives are connected to results in different lives. For example, if you commit some virtuous or negative actions in this life, then you will have to experience their results later on. Similarly, you may have committed some virtuous or unwholesome actions in a past life, whose results you will have to experience in that very life or in this life. If you have not accumulated such actions, then you will never experience their effects. On the other hand, if you have accumulated a particular action, then generally speaking you will never escape the result: sooner or later it will bear fruit. Similarly, if one has accumulated a positive action, the result will be definitely positive. Those kinds of actions are called definite actions, but there are also actions whose result is not very definite because the proper conditions or situations were not present. Furthermore, there are actions that seem of minor importance but whose results multiply rapidly depending on the circumstances, situation, and conditions. So there are many kinds of action—definite action, indefinite action, actions that multiply greatly—as well as the fact that the results of actions not done will not be encountered and that actions once done will not dissipate.

Usually all our daily actions arise from some wish or desire. For example, if you wish to go somewhere, you set out and go; if you wish to eat something, you look for something to eat and eat it. Desire can be classified into two types, one of which is negative and the other logical and creative. For example, the wish to attain liberation from cyclic existence results in a reasonable undertaking, therefore it is a sound and logical desire. On the other hand, to generate attachment toward a particular object, such that you wish to obtain or achieve something, is an impure desire and usually arises from a misconception of phenomena as existing independently or inherently. Most of the work that we do in cyclic existence, and the desires that we generate, is the result of this kind of illogical reasoning.

Familiarizing our minds with positive qualities and trying to achieve goals like liberation are logical desires. Still, it is possible that in particular cases an individual's wish to attain liberation is assisted by the conception of true existence. However, every wish for worldly perfection is based on the ignorance that conceives of true existence. On these grounds it is better to classify desire in two ways, one the result of correct reasoning and the other the result of incorrect reasoning.

The result of desire based on the conception of true existence is cyclic existence. Still, there is another kind of desire based on sound reasoning that does not project cyclic existence but aspires to attain the supreme attainments and qualities of the Buddha, the doctrine, the spiritual community, and nirvana, the state beyond suffering. There is a wish and desire to attain them.

If we do not classify desire into two types, we might think that desiring liberation was improper, that desiring religious practice was improper, and that even wishing for happiness was also improper. No doubt there are different modes of desiring your own happiness, but what is clear is that so long as we have attachment and a conception of a truly existent self, those actions characteristic of cyclic existence will continue to be created.

The Measure of Having Generated a Determination to Be Free

Generally speaking, once an action has been accumulated the result has to be experienced. Therefore, although we may be enjoying the delights of cyclic existence just now and intense sufferings are not manifest, since we are not free from the actions' shackles and snares, we have no security and no guarantee of lasting happiness. This is the perspective from which this particular text says,

**(5) Having familiarized yourself in this way,
if you do not generate admiration
for the prosperity of cyclic existence even
    for an instant,
and if you wish for liberation day and night,
at that time you have generated the
    determination to be free.**

By understanding the infallible law of actions and results you will be able to see that unless you completely purify your actions, whatever kind of apparent enjoyment and pleasure you find in cyclic existence will be unreliable. Having understood this, you will not be confused by the pleasures of cyclic existence and will be able to curb your attachment to the next life.

As human beings in cyclic existence, we normally encounter four kinds of suffering: the sufferings of birth, old age, sickness, and death. Right from birth we are faced with sufferings; our life begins with suffering. At the same time the process of aging begins and we start to encounter different degrees of sickness. Even when we are healthy we encounter a lot of disturbances and confusion. Finally, the chapter of our life is closed with the sufferings of death.

When we talk about someone who is in cyclic existence, we are referring to a sentient being who is uncontrollably under the sway of contaminated actions and delusions. Because we are overpowered by contaminated actions and delusions, we have to take repeated birth in a cycle; therefore it is called cyclic existence. Of the two, contaminated actions and delusions, it is delusions that are mainly responsible for casting us into cyclic existence. When we are free of delusions we attain liberation. Delusions are states of mind that, when they arise within our mental continuums, leave us disturbed, confused, and unhappy. Therefore those states of mind that delude or afflict us are called delusions or afflictive emotions. They are the negative qualities that make us unhappy when they arise within us. It is these internal disturbances and not external conditions that really make us suffer.

As long as we have those evildoers residing within us, happiness is impossible. So if we really want to transform ourselves and achieve maximum happiness, we must identify these deluded states of mind and eliminate them. Enlightenment, the state of greatest happiness, cannot be actualized by any other means than by transforming our minds. Usually, on an ordinary level, we think of delusions like attachment and anger as qualities that make life meaningful and vibrant. We think that without attachment and anger our whole society or community would become colorless and lifeless. But if you think carefully about it and weigh up the qualities and disadvantages of delusions like attachment and anger, you may find that in the short term they give you some relief and make your life seem eventful. But on closer scrutiny you will find that the fewer of these delusions we have, even though life may feel less urgent, we develop more inner calm, inner strength, and lasting happiness. Consequently, our minds will be happy, our physical health will improve, and we will be able to engage successfully in virtuous activities.

Of course, you might feel that your life now is colorless, unattractive, and without meaning. Yet if you look for your own and other sentient beings' long-term benefit and think carefully, you will notice that the more you control your delusions, the greater your peace of mind and physical well-being. In pursuit of physical health, many people do various kinds of yoga exercises. No doubt this is very good for them, but if they were also to do some mental yoga, that would be even better. In short, as long as your mind is disturbed and unsound, you will continue to encounter problems and sufferings. And as long as your mind is under control, disciplined, and free from these faults, you will gain more inner strength, calm, peace, and stability, as a result of which you will be able to be more creative. From our own experience—that we have more suffering when our minds are more disturbed by faults—we can deduce that when our minds are completely clear our experience of happiness will be stable.

Is Liberation Possible?

Up to this point we have been discussing the faults, sufferings, and delusions of cyclic existence. On the one hand, we have to think about the faults and sufferings of cyclic existence and generate aversion to them, and on the other, we need to ascertain the possibility of attaining nirvana—the cessation of suffering, the complete elimination of delusions. You might ask, is there really a method by which we can attain liberation or a method by which we will be able to eliminate sufferings and delusions completely? It would be worth asking first whether nirvana or liberation actually exists.

Liberation or cessation is the nature of the mind on the occasion of the complete annihilation of defilements by their antidotes. When you think about the sufferings of cyclic existence and you are weary of them, you look forward to nirvana, liberation, as an alternative. Let us say that we have a defiled and deluded mind. When the defilements of the previous moment of the continuum of this particular consciousness are completely eliminated, the very nature of that purified consciousness is liberation, nirvana, or true cessation. In other words, the teachings say that the cyclic existence that we are presently experiencing is not eternal because it has arisen from causes and conditions and they can be counteracted.

If you ask what is the cause of cyclic existence, it is ignorance, the conception of true existence. And what is the remedy for such ignorance? It is the wisdom realizing emptiness or the wisdom realizing the real nature of phenomena. Now these two qualities—ignorance, which is the cause of cyclic existence, and the wisdom realizing emptiness, which is the antidote to ignorance—cannot abide simultaneously in the continuum of one human being because they are mutually exclusive. Although both observe the same object, their modes of apprehension are completely opposed to each other. Therefore they cannot both abide in one person's continuum with equal strength. As one is strengthened, the other is weakened.

If you examine these two qualities carefully, you will find that whereas ignorance has no valid support or foundation, the wisdom realizing emptiness does. Any quality that has a valid foundation can be strengthened and developed limitlessly. On the other hand, because the conception of true existence lacks a valid foundation, when it encounters the wisdom realizing emptiness, a valid mind based on correct reasoning, it is weakened such that it can finally be eliminated altogether. So, ultimately, the wisdom realizing the nature of phenomena will be able to uproot ignorance, the source of cyclic existence.

If we examine how attachment and anger arise within us when our minds are calm and clear, in what way we crave the object, how it appears to us, and how we generate a conception of true existence toward it, we will be able to see how these delusions arise within us. Although we may not gain a direct understanding, we can make some correct assumptions.

How are attachment and anger supported by the conception of true existence? When, for example, you are very angry with somebody, notice how at that time you see that person as completely obnoxious, completely unpleasant. Then later a friend tells you, no, that person is not completely unpleasant because he has this or that quality. Just hearing these words, you change your mind and no longer see the person you were angry with as completely obnoxious and unpleasant. This clearly shows that right from the beginning, when you generate attachment, anger, and so forth, the mental tendency is to see that particular person or object not as merely pleasant or unpleasant but as completely unpleasant or completely pleasant. If the person is pleasant, you see him as completely attractive, 100 percent attractive, and if you are angry with him, you see him as completely unattractive. In other words, you see whatever quality they have as existing inherently or independently. Therefore this mode of apprehending phenomena as existing inherently or truly provides a strong basis for the arising of delusions like attachment and anger.

From such explanations, you can make an assumption that in general this quality—liberation or nirvana—does exist. It is a phenomenon. Not only does it exist but it is something that you can achieve within your mental continuum. If you train yourself in the twin practices of thinking about the disadvantages and sufferings of cyclic existence and the advantages of ridding yourself of these sufferings and the possibility of attaining liberation, then you will be able to generate a determination to become completely free from cyclic existence.

THE ROOT OF THE MIND OF ENLIGHTENMENT

The next verses explain the generation of the mind of enlightenment. First the need and purpose of generating altruism is explained.

**(6) If this determination to be free is not influenced
by a pure mind of enlightenment,
it will not become a cause for unsurpassable
   enlightenment, the perfect bliss;
therefore the intelligent should generate a
   mind of enlightenment.**

However strong your familiarity with the determination to be free of cyclic existence may be, unless you generate an altruistic attitude, a strong wish to benefit sentient beings, it will be impossible for you to attain enlightenment. In this regard Nagarjuna's *Precious Garland* says:

> If you and this world wish to actualize supreme
>   enlightenment,
> its root is the mind of enlightenment.

The basis for generating an altruistic aspiration for enlightenment is compassion, of which there are many types. One kind of compassion is to think how nice it would be if sentient beings were free from sufferings. There are other degrees of compassion that not only include this thought but also have greater courage. This induces a special resolve to take responsibility personally for getting rid of sentient beings' sufferings. Even the hearers and solitary buddhas strongly wish that sentient beings be separated from suffering. Similarly, we ourselves sometimes generate the kind of compassion that thinks how nice it would be if sentient beings were free from sufferings. For example, seeing the misery or neglected condition of a particular person or animal, we might generate a strong sense of compassion wishing that the sufferings of that particular sentient being be eliminated.

It is also important to note that when the object of our compassion is someone we like, our sympathy is based on attachment rather than compassion. On the other hand, if seeing the sufferings of a neglected animal, such as a stray dog to whom you have no attachment at all, you generate compassion, that is pure compassion.

Now the compassion generated by hearers and solitary buddhas is of a much higher quality than the compassion we normally generate, because, seeing the suffering that pervades the whole of cyclic existence, they generate compassion for all sentient beings. Unable to see the sufferings of all cyclic existence, we see only the sufferings of particular beings, which we see as some kind of fault or demerit in them. However, hearers and solitary buddhas do not have a compassion that induces them to take responsibility for liberating sentient beings themselves.

The compassion generated by bodhisattvas is of the highest kind. They not only wish that sentient beings be separated from suffering but also voluntarily take responsibility for ridding them of their sufferings. This is called great compassion. It is this compassion that underlies the altruistic aspiration for enlightenment and that induces the special attitude. For this reason we often come across statements in the scriptures that it is compassion that acts as the root of the mind of enlightenment. In order to generate such compassion, you must identify the suffering by which the particular sentient being is afflicted. You should also regard that being as pleasant and dear to your heart.

GENERATING THE MIND OF ENLIGHTENMENT

The seventh verse, along with the first two lines of the eighth verse, presents the method for cultivating the awakening mind.

> (7) Carried away by the four torrential rivers,
> bound by tight bonds of actions, difficult
>   to undo,
> caught in the iron net of the conception of
>   self,
> thoroughly enveloped by the thick darkness
>   of ignorance . . .
>
> (8a–b) born into boundless cyclic existence,
> and in rebirths unceasing tormented by the
>   three sufferings—
> contemplating the state of mother sentient
>   beings in such conditions, generate the
>   supreme mind.

The words "mother sentient beings" here clearly show that suffering sentient beings are not totally unrelated to you. They have acted as your mother in many previous lives and have been extremely kind to you. Therefore you should see them as very pleasing. Understanding how your mothers suffer will provoke in you a feeling of being unable to bear it. Through the mental process of recognizing how you are intimately connected to sentient beings, you will be able to generate the great compassion that gives rise to the mind of enlightenment. This verse says that sentient beings are carried away by four torrential rivers. These four could refer to the four causes that project sentient beings into birth in cyclic existence and they could also refer to their four results. Here the four rivers refer to the four unwanted sufferings that we encounter in cyclic existence: birth, aging, sickness, and death. In other words, we are completely under the control of very strong, irreversible, contaminated actions, because of which we experience these four sufferings.

Such strongly contaminated actions also arise from potent delusions like anger and attachment. These in turn arise from the powerful conception of (a truly existent) self. This phenomenon is compared to a strong iron net, due to which we are ensnared in cyclic existence. A strong conception of self means that it is stable and unchallenged. The stronger the conception of self is, the stronger delusions like anger and attachment will be. The stronger the delusions are, the stronger the actions that project us into cyclic existence will be. And the stronger the actions that project us into cyclic existence are, the more powerful our sufferings will be.

The misconception of self arises because we are obscured on all sides by the darkness of ignorance. In this context, the misconception of self that entraps us in cyclic existence refers to the misconception of self of persons, because the next line says that sentient beings are completely confused and enshrouded by the great darkness of ignorance. Usually the misconception of self itself is referred to as ignorance, but when we find two things explained, like the misconception of self and ignorance, the first, the misconception of self, refers to the misconception of self of persons, and ignorance in the next line refers to the misconception of self of phenomena, the misconception of phenomena as truly existent.

Our misconception of the true existence of phenomena, in other words, our strong grasping for the attraction of our physical body, acts as the foundation for generating too much attachment toward our own person. Therefore the misconception of phenomena acts as a foundation for the misconception of the person. When you observe the "I" in your continuum and generate a feeling of "I," a conception of a truly existent self—that is called the view of the transitory collection. So the misconception of self of phenomena gives rise to this view of the transitory collection, and this in turn stimulates the accumulation of actions. And because of the misconception of self of phenomena and the misconception of self of persons, we involuntarily take birth in cyclic existence and for an immeasurable time experience an unceasing chain of suffering, like birth, aging, sickness, and so forth.

Now the cessation of subsequent results depends on the cessation of the preceding causes. If strong causes have been created, then you have to experience their results, no matter how reluctant you are. If you think in this way, then the more you resent your sufferings the more you will loathe their causes. These verses explain two ways of generating renunciation and a determination to be free through thinking about true suffering: these are to think about the faults and sufferings of cyclic existence and to reflect on the true origins of suffering. When the verse explains the four levels of sufferings and so forth, it is explaining true suffering, and when it explains factors like the conception of true existence, ignorance, and contaminated action, it is explaining the true origins of suffering. In this way, it explains the first two noble truths.

If you think about this cycle of suffering and its origins with reference to other sentient beings, it will lead to training in compassion. But if you think about these sufferings and their origins with reference to yourself, it leads to the generation of a determination to be free.

Yesterday we were discussing the different levels of suffering and how to generate an altruistic attitude wishing to benefit all sentient beings. In this context, the text says:

> **(8c–d) Seeing the sufferings of the mother
>   sentient beings that are in such a
>   situation,
> we should generate the supreme mind.**

In other words, we must first observe the sufferings of sentient beings and then generate a strong feeling of closeness and affection for them. The closer you feel to other sentient beings the easier it will be to generate the feeling of being unable to bear their sufferings. Therefore we should view all sentient beings as our relatives, such as our mother.

In order to generate this mental attitude of concern for other sentient beings, we must first understand the beginningless nature of cyclic existence. The sentient beings who have taken birth in cyclic existence are also beginningless, therefore there is no sentient being who you can say has not been connected to you as a relative, such as your mother.

In order to generate a strong sense of affection and closeness to all sentient beings, you must first generate a strong sense of equanimity toward all sentient beings. Based on this feeling, you can generate a sense of kinship with all sentient beings and view them as your mother. Then you will be able to reflect kindness for these sentient beings, which is the same as kindness for your present family that sustains you now. When you see all sentient beings as your own relatives and remember their kindness, you will be able to generate an attitude of cherishing them, taking them to your heart.

Another method of generating an altruistic attitude is to exchange yourself with others. This is possible because all other sentient beings are the same as you in wanting happiness and not wanting suffering. They are also the same as you in having the capacity and the opportunity to get rid of suffering and attain happiness. Like you, all sentient beings have the right to eliminate suffering and attain maximum happiness. So you are the same from all these perspectives, and though all other sentient beings are countless, you are not unrelated to them because in worldly terms you are very much dependent on them. Even when you meditate on the path, you do so by focusing on sentient beings. Finally, ultimate enlightenment known as the effortless spontaneous achievement of others' purposes is achieved in dependence on them. Thus we are related to and dependent on sentient beings when we are in cyclic existence, during the path, and finally at the time of the fruit of the path.

Now, seeing that you have this close connection with all other sentient beings, it is foolish to neglect their welfare to pursue the interests of only one being—yourself. On the other hand, it is wise to neglect the interests of one for the benefit of the rest who are the majority of sentient beings. All the pleasures and facilities that we enjoy in this life, such as wealth, possessions, fame, and friendship, are all obtained in dependence on other beings. We cannot think of enjoying anything by our own efforts alone without their help. In this modern age especially, everything we enjoy—food, clothing, and everything else—is produced by various manufacturing companies in which other people work. Almost nothing is grown or produced in your own small garden or courtyard.

We eat tinned fruit that is produced by the hands of other human beings. When we travel in an airplane, we depend on the work and facilities provided by the many people who are involved in running that airplane. In our modern society we cannot think of surviving without depending on other human beings. Equally, without other human beings you would have neither reputation nor fame. Even though you may have acquired certain qualities that are the basis of your fame and reputation, if other people do not know about them there is no question of your becoming famous.

If you think carefully, even your enemy, whom you usually view as an opponent and dislike completely, gives you the chance to generate many qualities like patience, courage, and strength. There is a teaching by Shantideva in his chapter on patience that is pertinent here about how to generate patience with respect to your enemy and regard him as precious. This is especially important for a Buddhist practitioner. If you are able to see how you can gain these good qualities from your enemy, you will also be able to generate kind feelings toward him.

If you are able to generate such a positive mind toward your enemy, who is normally an object of contempt, you will have no trouble in generating a feeling of care and concern toward neutral beings or of course toward your friends. In order to generate such a mental attitude, it is not necessary that you recognize all the sentient beings individually. You can, for example, infer that all trees have certain common characteristics from the qualities of one particular tree without having to know each and every individual tree. Similarly, you can conclude that all living beings are the same in wanting happiness and not wanting suffering by examining your own situation. By doing so, you will easily generate compassion, which is an aspiration thinking how nice it would be if all sentient beings could eliminate suffering. If you are able to generate a clear understanding of the sufferings of sentient beings, you will also be able to generate love, which is to think how nice it would be if all sentient beings met with happiness.

Based on these two aspirations—love and compassion—you will generate the special attitude of taking responsibility for getting rid of these sufferings yourself, and this will induce the mind that wishes to attain the highest enlightenment for the sake of all sentient beings. This altruistic aspiration for enlightenment for the sake of all sentient beings is called the mind of enlightenment. The way to measure your generation of the mind of enlightenment and determination to be free was explained earlier.

THE NEED TO REALIZE EMPTINESS

From this point on, the text explains the nature of emptiness and the wisdom that realizes it. The first verse explains the need to generate this wisdom realizing the nature of emptiness. There are various kinds of wisdom: wisdom understanding conventional phenomena, such as the various sciences, and wisdom understanding the ultimate, real nature of phenomena. If you do not possess wisdom realizing the ultimate mode of existence, no matter how strong your determination to be free or your aspiration for enlightenment may be, you will not be able to shift your conception of true existence, the root cause of cyclic existence. Therefore you should make an effort to realize dependent arising.

> **(9) Without the wisdom realizing the ultimate nature of existence,**
> **even though you familiarize yourself with the determination to be free and the mind of enlightenment,**
> **the root of cyclic existence cannot be cut; therefore make an effort to realize dependent arising.**

Common explanations of the meaning of dependent arising, such as the dependent arising of cause and effect, are accepted by all Buddhist traditions. But this verse refers to subtle dependent arising, something coming into existence in dependence on its parts. In other words, there are conditioned relations in which particular effects or phenomena arise merely in dependence on a particular cause and condition. Another meaning of dependent arising is the existence of things relative to others. For example, when we talk about a part of a whole body, we call it a part in relation to the whole; similarly, the whole is only a whole in relation to its parts. From this point of view, the part and whole are related to and dependent on each other. Likewise, qualities like long and short have a relative sense because we use these terms to describe objects in relation to other objects.

At another level, phenomena are also called dependent arising because they arise in dependence on their basis of designation and they are dependent on the mind that designates them. The first meaning of dependent arising applies only to conditioned phenomena, whereas the last two meanings apply to all phenomena—conditioned impermanent phenomena and unconditioned permanent phenomena.

The dependent arising referred to in this line is the subtlest one, in which it is explained in terms of existing merely by name and designation by thought. In other words, when we say that phenomena exist through the power of terms and designations and in dependence on designations, we are explaining dependent arising as it appears, as mere existence due to the power of name. From the ultimate point of view, that is mere emptiness of inherent existence. This means that since a phenomenon cannot come into being from its own side, it lacks inherent existence and is dependent on other conditions. Here other conditions refer to designation and the designating thought. The phenomenon exists merely by the power of that designation, and as such it is empty of self-sufficient existence. Conversely, since it is empty of self-sufficient existence it exists through the power of designation.

So these are explanations of subtle emptiness. When we talk about the meaning of emptiness, we are talking about something being empty of its object of negation. Phenomena are empty of independent existence, inherent existence, and existence from their own side. These three—independent existence, inherent existence, existence from its own side—are the objects of negation.

Emptiness thus means being empty of these objects of negation. This is said because phenomena are dependent on something else, they are dependent on the name and the thought by which they are designated.

When we explain that phenomena are dependent on their parts, name, and designation, we are stating that they do not have inherent existence, because dependence and independence are opposite terms. Phenomena are either dependent or independent, they cannot be both. Since these terms are mutually exclusive, a phenomenon can only be one or the other, and not something in between. On the other hand, "human being" and "horse" are opposites but not direct opposites, because there can be a third category, such as "dog," that is neither horse nor human being. But "human being" and "nonhuman being" are direct opposites, and if we say that there are only two categories of phenomena, those that are either "human being" or "nonhuman being," there cannot be a third category. So by the reasoning of depending arising, lack of inherent existence can be established.

When we use the term "emptiness," it has some similarity to our usual idea of the absence of something or voidness. But if you think that emptiness is the mere absence of anything, then your understanding is incomplete. We should understand emptiness as the absence of inherent existence. Because they lack inherent existence, phenomena do not have an independent existence, yet they are existent. This understanding of emptiness can be gained by understanding the meaning of dependent arising because dependent arising means that phenomena are dependent on something else. They do not exist independently, nor do they exist from their own side. If phenomena exist in dependence on something else, this clearly shows that they do exist.

Sometimes emptiness is explained as the meaning of the middle way, which means the center that has eliminated the two extremes. One extreme is to think that if phenomena do not exist inherently, they do not exist at all—this is the extreme of nihilism. The other extreme is to think that if phenomena exist, they must exist inherently—this is the extreme of eternalism. If we have a good understanding of emptiness, on the one hand, we will understand that since phenomena exist in dependence on thought and name and so on, they have a nominal existence—that is to say, they do exist. This avoids the extreme of nihilism. On the other hand, when you think about how phenomena exist in dependence on thought and name, it is clear that they do not have an independent existence. This avoids the extreme of eternalism. If it were something that did not exist at all, then to say that it depended on something else would not make any sense.

The next verse clarifies and points to the need to generate the wisdom realizing emptiness.

> **(10) One who sees the infallible cause and effect**
> **of all phenomena in cyclic existence and beyond**

**and destroys all perceptions (of inherent
   existence)
has entered the path that pleases the Buddha.**

This means that if you are able to clearly ascertain and assert the infallibility of dependent arising, and if, without doing harm to this understanding of dependent arising, you are able to destroy the perception that things exist inherently, then you have entered the path that pleases the Buddha. The first two lines introduce the assertion that if you understand cause and effect within and beyond cyclic existence as infallible, and can posit the existence and function of cause and effect, rather than its nonexistence, then you are able to eliminate the extreme of nihilism. The next two lines imply that through understanding the function of cause and effect, you will understand that although things exist, they do not exist independently or inherently, and thus you will be able to destroy the conception that things exist inherently.

So these lines explain that although cause and effect functions, it does not function in an inherent way. In fact, inherent existence is the object of negation and is destroyed by true perception. This eliminates the extreme of permanence. In general, the whole of Buddhist teaching can be subsumed under four statements: all conditioned phenomena are impermanent, all contaminated things are suffering, all phenomena are empty and do not have self-existence, and nirvana is peace. From these four, it is clear that most schools of Buddhism, with the exception of certain subschools such as the Vatsiputriyas, accept the Buddhist explanation of selflessness.

The selflessness that is accepted by all four schools is the lack of a self-supporting or self-sufficient person—meaning, there is no person who is completely independent of the mental and physical aggregates. If you view the mental and physical aggregates as the subject to be controlled and the person as the controller, and if you view this controller, a person, as something completely independent of those aggregates, you are maintaining a false view of the existence of a substantial, self-supporting person.

All four tenet schools of Buddhism accept that there is no such person independent of her physical and mental aggregates. This understanding weakens our strong yearning for the person, the enjoyer of happiness and suffering, to be something solid, but it seems that it is not very effective in weakening the attachment, anger, and so on that is generated by observing other objects of enjoyment. In general, attachment, hatred, and so on, which are generated in relation to ourselves, are stronger, so we think of "my" object of enjoyment, "my" relative, or "my" rosary.

If the object of enjoyment does not belong to you, then you may not have a very strong sense of an independent, self-supporting person, but if you possess something, then that feeling is stronger. This is clear if you compare the two attitudes before and after buying something, let us say a watch. First you buy it, then you start thinking "this is my watch" and "these are my clothes" and so forth. Because of that feeling of "mine," the feeling of possessing a thing, you generate a very strong sense of the person to whom it belongs. Such a person is called a substantially self-sufficient person. If you talk about the nonexistence of such a substantially self-sufficient person to people who have a strong sense of the existence of such a person, it will help reduce their attachment to their possessions.

In addition to this explanation of the selflessness of persons, when we study the highest tenet schools—that is, the Mind Only and Middle Way schools—we find subtler explanations of the selflessness of not only persons but also phenomena. With respect to the Mind Only school's explanation, when we relate to different objects of enjoyment, such as form and sound, they appear to us owing to the awakening of imprints on our consciousness. So, according to the Mind Only explanation, all the various phenomena appear to us and we experience and enjoy them merely because of the awakening of the imprints left on the mind. In other words, all phenomena are of the nature of the mind and do not have any external existence.

This is one explanation of emptiness and is a means to reduce attachment toward objects of enjoyment. But the Middle Way explanation is that no phenomena, whether the person, the enjoyer, or the object of enjoyment, exist inherently from their own side, because they are merely designated by thought. Thought designates name and then the phenomenon comes into being. Phenomena do not have an existence from their own side, other than being designated by the terms and thoughts of the mind. According to this explanation, all phenomena have their own character and their own nature, but all these characteristics of specific phenomena exist in dependence on something else, they do not have a specific mode of existence from their own side.

Within the Middle Way school there are two interpretations of emptiness. According to the Middle Way Autonomy school, all phenomena exist, but their existence comes about as a product of two conditions. On the one hand, a valid mind should designate the name and the term to that particular phenomenon, and at the same time the phenomenon should also exist from its own side. When these two conditions are met, the phenomenon comes into existence. However, other than being designated by the mind, there are no phenomena that come forth from their own side.

The subtlest explanation is found in the Middle Way Consequentialist school, which says that although there are things like form, sound, mountain, house, and so forth that we can point to, they do not exist in the way we ordinarily perceive them. Usually phenomena appear to our consciousness as if they existed from their own side, but the Consequentialists say phenomena do not exist from their own side at all. They have only a conventional and a nominal existence. Therefore if phenomena exist in the way they appear to us, when we try to find, examine, and analyze the object of designation, it should become clearer and clearer. But this is not so. When we try to examine and analyze the nature of phenomena we have perceived, we are unable to find them; instead they disappear. This shows that phenomena do not have any inherent existence and do not exist from their own side.

According to the Autonomy school, the measure by which to prove that things exist is existence from their own side. But the Consequentialists say things do not exist from their own side at all because they are merely designated by the mind. For them a phenomenon's existence from its own side is the object of negation, and the lack of such inherent existence or existence from its own side is the meaning of emptiness.

If you are able to perceive the real nature of phenomena by realizing that they do not exist inherently but only in dependence on causes and conditions, such as designation by name and thought, you will have entered the path pleasing the Buddha. Usually when an object, form, or sound appears to us, it appears as if it has an independent or solid existence not dependent on causes, conditions, names, thoughts, and so forth. But that is not its real mode of existence. Therefore if you understand that phenomena exist in dependence on these things and you thereby eliminate the misunderstanding that they exist independently, you have understood the right path.

On the other hand, you might think about how all phenomena appear and the infallibility of their dependent arising but be unable to generate the realization that they are empty of inherent existence. Or when you think about the emptiness of phenomena or their lack of inherent existence, you might be unable to accept the infallibility of their dependent arising. When you have to alternate these two understandings and are unable to think of them simultaneously, you have not yet realized the thought of the Buddha. As the following verse says:

> (11) Appearances are infallible dependent arisings;
> emptiness is free of assertions.
> As long as these two understandings are seen as separate,
> one has not yet realized the intent of the Buddha.

Although phenomena do not have inherent existence, they have nominal existence. When we see the reflection of our own face in the mirror, the reflection is not the face itself. In other words, the reflection is empty of the real face. Even though the reflection of the face is not the face, the reflection of the face arises. The reflection is completely empty of being the real face and yet it is very much there. It was produced by causes and conditions and it will disintegrate due to causes and conditions. Similarly, phenomena have a nominal existence, although they have no existence independent of causes and conditions.

If you examine yourself or any other phenomena carefully in this way, you will find that although all phenomena appear to exist inherently, no phenomena exist from their own side or as they appear to us. However, they do have nominal existence that produces results, is functional, and whose activities are infallible.

> (12) At the time when these two realizations
>   are simultaneous and don't have to
>   alternate,
> from the mere sight of infallible dependent
>   arising comes ascertainment
> that completely destroys all modes of
>   grasping;
> at that time, the analysis of the profound
>   view is complete.

If you familiarize your mind with this insight, a time will come when you do not have to alternate the two understandings: the understanding of the meaning of dependent arising and that of emptiness of inherent existence. Then you will understand the meaning of emptiness of inherent existence by merely understanding the meaning of dependent arising without relying on any other reason. Merely by seeing that dependent arising is infallible, you will be able to destroy completely the misconception of the true existence of phenomena without relying on other conditions. When you are able to generate an understanding of dependent arising or emptiness of inherent existence as meaning the same thing, you have gained a complete comprehension of the view of the real nature of phenomena.

☙❧

We will now complete the remaining text of the *Three Principal Aspects of the Path*. When we think about a phenomenon's lack of inherent existence, we should start our investigation with our own person and try to find out whether this "I" or person has inherent existence or not. Find out who the person is and separate out the whole physical and consciousness aggregate by asking whether my brain is me, or my hand is me, or whether the other parts of the body are me. When analyzed in this way, then the "I" is unfindable. You cannot identify the "I" with any of these factors, neither the whole physical body, nor parts of it, nor consciousness and its various levels.

If you think about the physical body itself and try to find out what it is, whether it is the hand and so forth, it will be unfindable. Similarly, if you analyze a particular table to find out what it is, whether it is its color or its shape or the wood of which it is made, you will not be able to point to any particular quality of the table as the table.

When you are not able to find things through this mode of analysis, it does not mean that they do not exist. That would contradict reason and your own experience. Phenomena's unfindability under scrutiny indicates that they do not have any objective existence from their own side and that they exist as posited or designated by the mind. There is no other way of establishing them. Since they do not have any objective existence independent of thought, their existence is dependent on the power of the object, the designation. Therefore phenomena have a conventional or nominal existence.

When you are not analyzing or experimenting or studying in that particular manner and phenomena appear to you in their usual way, they appear to exist independently from their own side. It does not appear to you that they have only a nominal or conventional existence. But since you have some understanding through analysis and study, when things ordinarily appear to you as existing independently, you will be able to think, "Although phenomena do not have inherent existence, to my impure mind they appear to exist independently and inherently." In other words, if as a result of your study you compare phenomena's ordinary mode of appearance with the way things appear under investigation, you will understand the wrong way in which phenomena appear when you are not analyzing them, and then you will be able to identify the object of negation, inherent existence.

Therefore, when you are in a meditation session, it is important to ascertain through reasoning that things exist merely by designation and do not have an independent existence from their own side. However, as soon as you arise from meditation things will appear in the ordinary way. Then, due to the understanding you generated during the meditation session, even though phenomena appear as if they exist inherently or independently, you will be able to confirm that although they appear in this way, this is not how they exist.

It is from this point of view that the next verse says:

(13) Also, when the extreme of existence is eliminated by appearances,

and the extreme of nonexistence is
     eliminated by emptiness,
and the nature of the arising of cause and
     effect from emptiness is known,
you will not be captivated by the view
     that grasps at extremes.

This means that if you are able to understand that all phenomena exist conventionally, you will be able to eliminate the extreme of permanence, and by understanding
that things do not have inherent existence, you will be
able to eliminate the extreme of total nihilism or annihilation. In other words, you will be able to understand the
nature of phenomena, that they exist conventionally and
nominally but are empty of inherent existence. Because
of their not existing inherently, things appear as causes
and effects. If you are able to generate an understanding
of such a mode of existence, you will not be overpowered
or captivated by the wrong view of the two extremes—
that is, permanence and nihilism.

Finally, the concluding verse says:

(14) Thus when you have realized the
     essentials
of the three principal aspects of the path,
     accordingly,
seek solitude and generate the power of
     effort,
and quickly actualize your ultimate purpose,
     my son.

The concluding advice is that it is not enough to have mere scriptural understanding. Having understood the meaning of the three principal aspects of the path, it is your responsibility to retire to an isolated place and put them sincerely into practice. Having understood the meaning of practice, you must engage in it with clarity. The aim and purpose of study is the attainment of omniscience, but it can only be gained through practice. So Jé Tsongkhapa advises us to practice well.

Therefore, as explained above, first establish some understanding of the view that phenomena lack inherent existence, then repeatedly make your mind familiar with that understanding so that through familiarity your ascertainment will become clearer, deeper, and stabler. Moreover, as our mind at present is strongly influenced by distraction and excitement, it is very difficult for it to stay calmly on one object even for a short time. Under such conditions, even if you have realized the ultimate view, it is difficult to make it manifest.

In order to have a direct perception of emptiness it is important to develop a calmly abiding mind through meditation. There are two techniques for doing so: one accords with the explanation you find in the sutras, and the other, which is found in the tantras, depends on deity yoga. This latter method is the more profound. In the tantras too, there are two levels, according to the deity yoga found in the lower classes of tantra and in the highest class of tantra.

In the Highest Yoga Tantra there is a special mode of doing deity yoga and achieving a calmly abiding mind by employing the subtle wind and the subtle mind. When you actualize calmly abiding mind through that process, what is known as a union of calm abiding and special insight into emptiness is achieved.

If we explain this union of special insight and calm abiding merely according to the nature of the meditative stabilization, there is no certainty that it will become a cause of enlightenment. No doubt because of the attainment of special insight it is a Buddhist practice, but it is less certain that the mere union of calm abiding and special insight will become a cause of enlightenment. Whether it becomes a cause of liberation or omniscience depends on the motivation. Therefore we need a determination to be free from cyclic existence as a foundation, and then, based on care and concern for the benefit of all sentient beings, an altruistic aspiration for enlightenment. If you then practice the yoga of the union of special insight and calmly abiding mind, it will become an active force for attaining enlightenment.

In order for such practice to be fruitful, it is important that you first receive tantric teachings. In order to receive tantric teachings to ripen your mental continuum, you must first receive initiation to make your mind fertile. Therefore it is important to practice a combination of method and wisdom. When we engage in the altruistic aspiration to attain enlightenment for the sake of all sentient beings, it will influence and support the view understanding the real nature of phenomena, and in turn our realization of emptiness, the real nature of the phenomena, will also influence and support our aspiration for enlightenment. This mode of practice is known as the union of method and wisdom.

When you follow the tantric path, you first generate a mind wishing to attain enlightenment for the sake of all sentient beings, and then, influenced by this altruistic aspiration, you generate the wisdom realizing emptiness, the real nature of phenomena, and on the basis of this realization you generate the deity. In other words, it is the wisdom apprehending the emptiness itself that is generated into the form of a deity. If you again focus on the nature of the deity itself, you will find that even the deity does not exist from its own side. Then you visualize the deity as the truth body that you will ultimately attain when you attain enlightenment.

So the technique for meditating on both method and wisdom is very important and includes meditation on the extensive circle of the deity as well as on its profound emptiness. The unity of both method and wisdom is involved in this tantric practice, because, on the one hand, you think about the nature of the deity itself, which is visualizing the real nature of phenomena, and then on the other hand, you think of the deity itself as the truth body that you will attain when you become enlightened, which is to think about the object of your attainment. So this is also a meditation on the aspiration for enlightenment.

Through the process of deity yoga you are practicing the method and wisdom at the same time. This is what makes the path so quick and successful. When you follow the Highest Yoga Tantra especially, there are techniques to make manifest the subtlest wind and subtlest consciousness. Through special techniques you will be able to stop the coarser, defiled levels of wind and consciousness and make their subtlest levels manifest.

Whether you follow the sutra or tantra path, if you want to practice in this way, you should first establish a solid foundation in the practice of morality or discipline.

There are many levels of discipline to be observed, starting from the discipline of individual emancipation, which is like the foundation of all the higher levels of discipline. It is sometimes referred to as the discipline of the hearers, and it is on the basis of this that you generate the discipline of the bodhisattva, on the basis of which in turn you generate the discipline of mantra.

Part 4

Questions and Answers

Would Your Holiness clarify whether the determination to achieve liberation is not linked at all with the conception of true existence or the conception of phenomena as inherently existent?

Usually when we talk about generating a strong wish to be free from cyclic existence, a mind wishing to attain liberation, with reference to a person who has understood through study that there is such a thing as liberation and that it is something that can be achieved, and who has a deep understanding based on reason, then we can say that his wish to attain liberation is not defiled by a conception of true existence or a conception of phenomena as inherently existent. This is because a person can usually have a valid cognition of liberation only after realizing emptiness. If you have understood the meaning of emptiness, then even though you may not have uprooted the conception of true existence completely, neither the liberation that has to be established nor the path that establishes it are polluted by the conception of true existence or the conception of phenomena as inherently existent.

However, in the case of ordinary beings like us, who do not have a correct or authentic understanding of liberation's mode of existence, but merely a wish to attain it, while no doubt the wish is genuine, due to not understanding the real nature of phenomena, we might see liberation itself as truly or inherently existent. In other words, not having a good understanding of phenomena's lack of inherent existence, the wish to attain liberation is polluted by the conception of true existence.

In a verse of sutra the Buddha says that if on see-ing the illusory image of a beautiful woman you feel a desire for her, it is foolish to regret it later when you realize that she was only an illusion, because there was no woman there in the first place. Similarly, if you think of liberation as truly existent, although it is not, then it is true to say that your aspiration toward liberation is not authentic.

Can we use a term like the "bliss of liberation"?

Yes, of course, because when we attain liberation, it is only the complete cessation of delusions. Otherwise one is still a person with a physical body. There is a feeling of pleasure and happiness of having attained liberation, although there is no craving for that blissful feeling. For example, if we speak in tantric terms, then a superior individual being who has eliminated the conception of true existence has the wisdom of great bliss within her mental stream and that bliss is a real bliss. I think it is also appropriate to speak of the bliss of an individual at the stage of no longer training. So we can say that even the Buddha has a feeling of pleasure, and therefore we can speak of the bliss of liberation.

But if you are asking this question from the point of view of whether liberation itself is bliss, then it is not because it is an impersonal phenomenon. Actually, lib-eration or cessation is a quality, a complete cessation of delusion within the particular person who has attained and actualized liberation. With reference to that person and when she attains liberation, it is the person herself who experiences bliss. So, if you ask whether the person experiences the bliss of liberation, the answer is yes, but if you ask whether liberation itself is bliss, then the answer is negative.

How is meditation related to getting rid of the suffering of sentient beings?

When a bodhisattva engages in training prior to enlightenment, he not only meditates on qualities like compassion and altruism but he also engages in putting the six perfections into practice. Of the six perfections, giving and ethical discipline are directly related to the benefit of sentient beings. Similarly, a bodhisattva also engages in the four means of gathering disciples, such as giving things that sentient beings need, speaking pleasantly, and so forth. The generation of compassion and love in meditation generates the intention and the practice of giving, observing ethical discipline, and so on, which are the expression of that intention in action. Therefore practical application and meditation work together side by side. You will also find mention of the state of equipoise and the subsequent achievement. During meditative equipoise you engage in meditation, and during the postmeditative state you arise from meditation and engage in collecting merit. This means practically engaging in activities that directly benefit sentient beings.

How is one's aspiration toward liberation related to the experiences of suffering?

In order to generate a wish to attain liberation, you should first be able to see the faults of cyclic existence. But at the same time, if you do not have an understanding of the possibility of attaining liberation, then merely seeing the faults and sufferings of cyclic existence is not enough. There are many cases where people are faced with suffering but are unaware of the possibility of attaining liberation. Not finding a solution to their problems, in frustration they commit suicide or harm themselves in other ways.

When the hearer and the solitary buddhas have destroyed delusions completely and become foe destroyers, do they possess a neutral consciousness or neutral mind?

Yes, they have a neutral consciousness. After having attained the status of a foe destroyer, the hearers and solitary buddhas not only have a neutral consciousness but also employ other qualities, like harsh speech and referring to others as inferior persons and so on. Although these kinds of actions are not provoked by delusions like anger and attachment, they arise as a result of being well-acquainted with negative qualities in the past, which now expresses itself physically, verbally, and mentally in bad ways.

People who have not realized emptiness see all phenomena as existing inherently, and because of that they generate anger, attachment, and so forth. But how do those people who have realized emptiness generate anger and attachment, since the realization of emptiness is a direct antidote to the conceptual experience of true existence?

To demarcate these two experiences: those who have realized emptiness do not have a conception of true existence that views things as inherently existent. Although things appear to them as inherently existent, they do not have a conception of true existence. Things appear to exist inherently even to those who have attained higher grounds and become foe destroyers. Yet there is no certainty that those persons for whom things appear to exist inherently should have attachment and anger. Anger and other delusions are generated not simply when things appear to exist truly but when there is also a determination that things have true existence. It is not possible to eliminate delusions and afflictions completely, merely by seeing emptiness or merely realizing selflessness. You have to realize emptiness or selflessness and also become well acquainted with it. When you understand emptiness and see it directly, you attain what we call the path of seeing. And when you attain the path of seeing, you are able to temporarily suppress all superficial manifestations of delusions. Still you have only suppressed the manifestations of these delusions and have not finally eliminated their seeds. The innate delusions are still present.

Even after you have gained a direct realization of emptiness there are higher paths, such as the path of seeing and the path of meditation. Intellectually acquired delusions are those that are eliminated by the path of seeing and are thus eliminated when one sees emptiness directly. They come about as a result of studying mistaken philosophical ideas. In other words, intellectually acquired delusions are product of wrong views. When you see emptiness or ultimate reality directly, naturally these delusions—products of wrong views—are automatically eliminated. Therefore you have to thoroughly realize the true nature of phenomena. Then gradually as you attain the path of meditation, you will be able to eliminate the very root cause of delusions.

Now, how is this conception of true existence, or the conception that things exist inherently, responsible for generating delusions like anger, attachment, and so forth? Normally speaking, it is not necessarily the case that whenever there is a conception of true existence delusions like attachment and anger are generated, because there are occasions when you have only a conception of true existence. But wherever there is attachment or anger, it follows that it is due to a conception of the true existence of phenomena. When you generate attachment, you not only see the object as interesting or attractive, you see it as something totally attractive, totally interesting, and existing inherently from its own side. Because of that kind of misconception of phenomena, you generate a strong attachment.

Similarly, when you see something as uninteresting or unattractive, you see it as totally uninteresting and unattractive. This is because you have a conception of the true existence of phenomena. The principal cause of all these different delusions, like attachment and anger, is the concept of "I" and "mine." First you generate attachment toward the "I," and because of this you start to generate all kinds of other delusions. Usually you do not think about what this "I" is, but when it arises automatically, you have a strong sense of an "I" that is not just nominally existent but is a solid "I" existing inherently from its own side.

Recognizing the existence of a conventional "I" is all right, but when you exaggerate it as having an independent existence it is wrong. That is the wrong view of transitory collection. Because you have a concept of the true existence of the "I," you generate other delusions, like the concept of "mine," thinking, "This or that is *mine*." When you have this conception of things as "mine" you divide everything into two classes: things that you like, which you think of as "mine," as interesting, as my friend, and so on, based on which you generate a lot of attachment, and things that do not belong to you or that have harmed you or are likely to harm you, which you classify into a different category and neglect them. Because of your concept of the "I" and the feeling that you are somehow supreme, someone very important, you become proud. Due to this pride, when you don't know something you generate deluded doubt, and when you encounter a challenge from people who have qualities or wealth similar to your own, you generate the delusions of jealousy and competitiveness toward them.

What is the meaning of a definite action and an indefinite action?

A definite action is when all of the requisite parts are complete. For example, making the preparations for doing a particular action, doing it, and finally thinking that you have done the right thing. If you have committed an action through such a process, the result will be definite, so it is called a definite action.

On the other hand, if you have not generated the intention to commit a particular action, then even if you have done something, the result will not be definite, so it is called an indefinite action. In general, there are many kinds of actions explained in Asanga's *Compendium of Abhidharma* (*Abhidharmasamuccaya*): actions that are committed and not accumulated, actions that are accumulated and not committed, and actions that are both committed and accumulated. Actions that are accumulated and not committed are definite actions. Actions that are committed and not accumulated are indefinite actions because, for example, of not being motivated.

Now, to explain this point more clearly, let us take the example of killing an animal. Generally speaking, killing leads to bad rebirth. But if you kill a particular animal without intending to kill it, for instance if you unknowingly trample on an insect and kill it, but then realizing what you have done you generate a strong sense of regret, the result will be indefinite. Because you have killed the insect you have committed the action of killing it, but you have not accumulated the action because you did not intend to kill it. In this case, the result is not definite, which means that this act of killing will not lead to the normal result, bad rebirth, because of the absence of intention and having subsequently felt regret. However, since the act of killing was committed, it will bear its own fruit. It does not lead to profit.

How is it possible, especially for a person who comes from the West, to generate a sense of renunciation, an unwillingness to enjoy the pleasures of the world in which we are living?

It is not likely that everyone will generate a spirit of renunciation, nor is it necessary, because of people's diverse mental interests and inclinations. Some take rather a fancy to cyclic existence. So what should we do? If we take the point of view of a Buddhist and strive to attain liberation, then we have to train the mind in this way. If you just glance at the Western way of life, you may see many superficial attractions, the ample modern facilities and so on. But if you examine it on a deeper level, Westerners are not immune to the general worldly sufferings of birth, old age, sickness, and death, and are especially stricken with feelings of competitiveness and jealousy. I am sure that these disturb your happiness, so they are termed the "sufferings of cyclic existence."

We can also classify suffering into three levels: the suffering of suffering, the suffering of change, and pervasive compositional suffering. The last one, pervasive compositional suffering, refers to the fact that our physical body, projected by contaminated actions and delusions, itself acts as the basis for experiencing all the different levels of suffering. It is important to know the various levels and stages of sufferings and how to do meditation. In general, if you have no anxiety, no troubles, and no worries, that is best. We think of practicing the Buddha's doctrine because we have some suffering, some anxiety, but if you don't have these, then there is no need to practice, just enjoy yourself.

Since we have this conception of a truly existent self, is it possible to benefit other beings?

It is possible. There are two kinds of mistaken attitudes with regard to the self: one is to hold it as inherently existent, the other is the self-centered attitude. If you have a very strong self-centered attitude, perpetually concerned about your own well-being and nothing else, you will automatically neglect the welfare of other beings. The conception of a truly existent self is difficult to get rid of, but while you are doing so you can also train in the altruistic attitude concerned with the welfare of other sentient beings and engage in activities to benefit them. Hearer and solitary foe destroyers have destroyed the delusions at the seed and have realized the ultimate nature of phenomena. They have eliminated the conception of true existence, but because of their self-centered attitude, they may not care much for the welfare of other sentient beings. However, it is also possible for a bodhisattva to belong to the Vaibhashika school, which does not assert the emptiness of true existence as one of its tenets. So although that bodhisattva may not have eliminated the seed of the conception of true existence, because he has trained in developing an attitude of concern for others, he will work with total dedication for the benefit of other sentient beings.

Bibliography

ABBREVIATIONS

Toh *The Tibetan Tripiṭaka*, Dergé edition, as described in H. Ui et al., eds., *A Complete Catalogue of the Tibetan Buddhist Canon*. Sendai, Japan: Tohoku University, 1934.

WORKS REFERENCED

Kangyur (Canonical Scriptures)

Tathāgata Essence Sūtra. Tathāgatācintyaguhanirdeśasūtra. De bzhin gshegs pa'i gsang ba bsam gyis mi khyab pa bstan pa'i mdo. Toh 47, dkon brtsegs *ka*.

Tengyur (Canonical Treatises)

Asanga. *Compendium of Abhidharma* (*Abhidharmasamuccayā*). *Chos mngon pa kun las btus pa.* Toh 4049, sems tsam *ri*.

Maitreya. *Sublime Science* (*Uttaratantra*). *Theg pa chen o rgyud bla ma.* Toh 4024, sems tsam *phi*.

Nagarjuna. *Fundamental Wisdom of the Middle Way* (*Mula-madhyamakakarika*). (A lucid English translation of this text can be found in Jay Garfield's *Fundamental Wisdom of the Middle Way.* New York: Oxford University Press, 1995.)

———. *The Precious Garland (Ratnavali). Rgyal po la gtam bya rin po che'i phreng ba.* Toh 4158, spring yig *ge.* (For an English translation of this text by John Dunne and Sara McClintock, see *The Precious Garland.* Boston: Wisdom Publications, 1997.)

Shantideva. *Guide to the Bodhisatta's Way of Life (Bodhisattvacaryavatara). Byang chub sems dpa'i spyod pa la 'jug pa.* Toh 3871, dbu ma *la.*

Tsongkhapa Losang Drakpa (Tsong kha pa Blo bzang grags a, 1357–1419). *The Great Stages of the Path. Byang chub lam rim che ba bzhugs so.* Taipei, Taiwan, ROC: Corporate Body of the Buddha Education Foundation, 2000.

———. *Three Principals of the Path. Lam gyi gsto bo rnam gsum gyi rtsa ba bzhugs so. Collected Works,* vol. *kha.*

About the Author

Tenzin Gyatso, His Holiness the Fourteenth Dalai Lama, was born in northeastern Tibet in 1935. Though he describes himself as "a simple monk," he is to many the very face of Buddhism today. He is the spiritual and temporal leader of the Tibetan people, a Nobel Peace Prize recipient, and a beacon of inspiration for Buddhists and non-Buddhists alike. He is committed not only to the teaching and practice of Buddhism but to inter-religious dialogue across political lines as well, and he also engages in dialogue with scientists in his mission to advance peace and understanding in the world. In doing so, he embodies his motto, "My religion is kindness." His Holiness resides today in Dharamsala, India, the site of the Tibetan government-in-exile.

A distinguished Buddhist scholar, Ven. Geshe Lhak-dor has served His Holiness the Dalai Lama as his translator and religious assistant since 1989, accompanying His Holiness to numerous conferences and forums worldwide. He has co-translated and co-produced several books by the Dalai Lama. Geshe is a trustee of the Foundation for Universal Responsibility, established by His Holiness. He is also the director of the Central Archive of His Holiness, a member of the Advisory Board of the Institute of Tibetan Classics in Montreal, Canada, and an Honorary Professor at the University of British Columbia, Canada. He is now the director of the Library of Tibetan Works and Archives and head of the Science Education Project.

Also Available from Wisdom Publications

A Lamp to Illuminate the Five Stages
Teachings on Guhyasamāja Tantra
Tsongkhapa
Translated by Gavin Kilty

The Life and Teachings of Tsongkhapa
Edited by Robert A. F. Thurman

The Middle Way
Faith Grounded in Reason
The Dalai Lama
Translated by Thupten Jinpa

The Splendor of an Autumn Moon
The Devotional Verse of Tsongkhapa
Translated and commentary by Gavin Kilty

Steps on the Path to Enlightenment
A Commentary on Tsongkhapa's Lamrim Chenmo
Geshe Lhundub Sopa

Tantric Ethics
An Explanation of the Precepts for Buddhist Vajrayāna Practice
Tsongkhapa
Translated by Gareth Sparham

Tsongkhapa's Praise for Dependent Relativity
Commentary by Lobsang Gyatso
Translated by Graham Woodhouse

About Wisdom Publications

Wisdom Publications is the leading publisher of classic and contemporary Buddhist books and practical works on mindfulness. To learn more about us or to explore our other books, please visit our website at wisdompubs.org or contact us at the address below.

Wisdom Publications
199 Elm Street
Somerville, MA 02144 USA

We are a 501(c)(3) organization, and donations in support of our mission are tax deductible.

Wisdom Publications is affiliated with the Foundation for the Preservation of the Mahayana Tradition (FPMT).